MRS MALAPROP LIVES

DES MacHALE

THE MERCIER PRESS

The Mercier Press, 4 Bridge Street, Cork
24 Lower Abbey Street, Dublin 1

ISBN 0 85342 966 9

Illustrations by Joseph Gervin

This book is dedicated to
JOHN and SIMON

Printed in Ireland by Litho Press Co. Midleton Co. Cork.

Mrs Malaprop Lives

INTRODUCTION

Mrs Malaprop is alive and well and living everywhere. Not literally, of course, but she survives in the persona of the many women and men who carry on her fine tradition of hilarious verbal blundering. The character of Mrs Malaprop first appears in *The Rivals*, a play by the Irish author Richard Brinsley Sheridan (1751–1816) written in 1775. The name seems to be derived from the French 'mal á propos' meaning an inopportune remark or ill to the purpose.

In plain language, a malaprop is the replacing of one word by another of like sound but radically different meaning which often conjures up a totally different image from the one intended. The best malaprops are those where the new unintended meaning is often a more appropriate description of the situation. For example Mrs Malaprop stated that her moth-eaten fur coat was bought at a 'jungle sale'. In general, the listener is aware of the malaprop but the speaker is not. Malaprops are an excellent illustration of Edgar Allan Poe's dictum —

A little learning is a dangerous thing

Malaprops occur most often with longer technical words derived from Latin or Greek. They are rife in medicine, science, literature and foreign languages and in fact in any technical area where the layman blunders in. The best profession for malapropists appears to be that of cleaning ladies. This is not a derogatory statement because malaprop's are highly creative and have more than a touch of genius about them.

Why do we find malaprops so funny? One reason is that they make us feel so superior — after all, we wouldn't make the silly verbal blunders poor Mrs Malaprop does — or would we? Secondly, they illustrate the extraordinary richness of language, revealing hidden connections between words and concepts, just as dreams do. Thirdly, very many of them are authentic, and reality has the uncanny knack of being a lot funnier than anything fiction can contrive. Finally, the malaprop is a first cousin of the Freudian slip, the bull, the blunder, the blooper, the boner, the howler, and the slip of the tongue, where many a true word is spoken in jest.

This book contains over six hundred malaprops — the biggest collection that has ever been assembled. Keep your ears open and you will hear many more of them, because Mrs Malaprop is living near you!

♣

Mrs Malaprop took a first-aid course and liked to try out her skills on real patients, so she got a job with the local ambulance service. One night she was called out in an emergency to an old man who had just been involved in a fire. Unfortunately, before the ambulance arrived, the old man died.

'What a pity I didn't arrive in time,' said Mrs Malaprop, 'or I could have resuffocated him and survived him.'

What did Mrs Malaprop say after her first helicopter flight?
It's good to be back on terracotta again.

Mrs Malaprop does not believe in the claims made by alternative medicine. In fact she is a confirmed septic on such matters.

Mrs Malaprop at prayer:
Blessed be the Holy Spirit the Parakeet.

Mrs Malaprop has been reading a very interesting book about General Rommel, the man who commanded Hitler's Pansy Division in North Africa.

7

Mrs Malaprop is sorry that her father hadn't been a surgeon because if he had, when she went to hospital she would get RIP treatment.

Mrs Malaprop has just been to see one of her favourite theatrical productions. It is called *Arsenal and Old Lace*.

Mrs Malaprop isn't exactly divorced from her husband but they don't really get along very well together. In fact she admits that they are enstrangled.

Mrs Malaprop had a big blank wall at the side of her house so to brighten up the area she had a muriel painted on it.

Mrs Malaprop's doctor once refused to treat her because she didn't have enough money to pay his fees. She told him that this behaviour was contrary to his hypocritical oath.

Mrs Malaprop has just been reading a newspaper article about a Soviet agent who defecated to the west.

Mrs Malaprop has just been reading a new biography about the famous Indian Prime Minister Bandit Nehru.

Mrs Malaprop's little daughter has just gone off

to boarding school for the first time, so she's put her entrails on her underwear.

Mrs Malaprop is convinced that her telephone bill is at least double the size it should be. She's got no satisfaction from the telephone company so she's going to write to the omnibusman.

Mrs Malaprop's father was an accomplished musician. He played the baboon in a sympathy orchestra.

Mrs Malaprop is not superstitious, but she reads her horrorscope every day in the newspaper.

Actually, Mrs Malaprop does not like the name Mrs Malaprop very much. She is thinking of having it changed by Interpol.

Mrs Malaprop went on holiday and received the greatest fright of her life. She was out swimming in the sea one day when an octopus came and wrapped his testicles around her.

Mrs Malaprop got a present of a bottle of Beaujolais for Christmas so she sent the following thank-you note to the donor:—
    'I am internally grapeful for the wine'.

Mrs Malaprop's cat has just died and she plans to bury it before vigour mortis sets in.

Mrs Malaprop feels that scientists should be given as much money as they need to build large lavatories in which they can do such important work.

Mrs Malaprop has decided not to attend any more political meetings. Last time she attended one, souffles broke out in the crowd.

Mrs Malaprop's daughter has been attending a cookery course in a famous French school of cuisine. She graduated top of the class and was awarded the condom bleu.

Mrs Malaprop put an end to her little boy's hobby of stamp collecting because she remembered the old proverb 'Philately will get you nowhere'.

Mrs Malaprop has just been in a big city hotel. What impressed her most was the revolting door at the front.

Mrs Malaprop is helping her daughter furnish her new house. She has just bought her a pelvis on which to hang her curtains.

From an early age Mrs Malaprop's son wanted to have a career in law enforcement, so he became a defective in the police farce.

For the cold winter months ahead, Mrs Malaprop has decided to invest in some terminal underwear.

MRS MALAPROP'S RELIGIOUS BELIEFS

Jesus was betrayed by Judas the carrycot.

Jesus was condemned by a bunch of spiders.

And the angel said 'take the child and flea into Egypt'.

The Pope lives in a vacuum.

At the last supper the apostles were filled with the Holy Spirit.

And the Lord said: 'Lay not up for yourselves trousers on earth'.

Jesus had a lady friend named Mary Mandolin.

Blessed art thou a monk's women.

And the angel said to Mary: 'Hail, highly flavoured one'.

And they brought him gifts of gold, frankenstein and myrrh.

And Mary was exposed to a man called Joseph.

Judas asparagus was one of Jesus' disciples.

Salami demanded the head of John the Baptist.

Jews worship in a cinemagogue.

The pope is inflammable.

In Greek Orthodox churches they burn insects.

The principal religion of Iran is muslin.

The Israelites spent forty years wandering in the dessert.

Jacob, the son of Isaac, stole his brother's birth-mark.

Joseph had a goat of many colours.

Solomon had five hundred wives and seven hundred cucumbers.

Catholics, after they die, are purified in purg-atives.

God spoke to Moses from a burning bus.

Salome danced naked in front of Harrods.

Pontius Pilot directed the flight into Egypt.

The Burial Service — In the name of the Father

and of the Son and into the hole he goes.

The first book of the bible is the Book of Guinnesses.

Round John virgin, Mother and child.

Angels lie prostate before the Lord.

Baby Jesus was persecuted by King Horrid.

It is not awful to marry your brother's wife.

Mrs Malaprop was worried by the smell from her drains so she sent for the sanity inspector.

Mrs Malaprop is spending a great deal of time in the bathroom at the moment. She has an attack of dire rear.

Mrs Malaprop's husband, who is a musician, went on strike recently and the entire orchestra came out in symphony.

There was a night watchman keeping guard over a hole in the road outside Mrs Malaprop's house one frosty night. But she didn't worry about him because he kept himself warm with a burning brassiere.

Mrs Malaprop is convinced that the name of the Irish parliament is Dole Éireann.

Mrs Malaprop's son and his girlfriend have just set out on a continental touring holiday on one of those tantrum bicycles.

Mrs Malaprop has given up arguing with her husband. She claims he is totally imprevious to logic.

The equator, Mrs Malaprop learned in geography, is a menagerie lion running around the middle of the earth.

Mrs Malaprop's son is planning a military career. He is planning to join the Gherkins in India.

Violence begets violence, Mrs Malaprop believes, and the whole thing becomes a viscous circle.

Mrs Malaprop once attended a dramatic production in which the costumes and makeup were particularly realistic. She remembers two actors dressed in the garbage of a monk who even went so far as to cut real tonsils on their heads.

Mrs Malaprop's uncle has just returned from the African jungle, full of the most wonderful antidotes about the natives.

Mrs Malaprop was very worried when she was told that her husband had a tuba on the brain but was relieved when she found out that it was non-militant.

Mrs Malaprop and her husband were holidaying in a hotel in Eastern Europe when an earthquake suddenly struck.
  'It was terrifying,' she told a reporter, 'when we went to bed, everything was perfectly still. And then when we woke up there beside us was a yawning abbess.'

JUDGE: 'Who is making these allegations?'
MRS MALAPROP: 'I am the alligator, your warship.'

Mrs Malaprop is very proud of her son's recent appointment. He has just been appointed an inspector in the Departure from Education.

Mrs Malaprop has just returned from a trip to Spain. The highlight of her visit was an exhibition of flamingo dancing.

Mrs Malaprop once found her little boy removing a buggy from his nose with his finger.

Mrs Malaprop is thinking of flying from London to Edinburgh on the new shuffle service.

Because she tends to gossip a bit, none of Mrs Malaprop's neighbours will speak to her. In fact they have ostrichised her.

Mrs Malaprop is very afraid of being attacked some dark night by a strange man, so she is taking a course in the marital arts.

Mrs Malaprop would love to take a keep-fit course because she fancies herself in one of those leopard outfits.

Mrs Malaprop had severe pains in her stomach so she went to the doctor. After a few tests he told her that she had ulsters.

Mrs Malaprop is very concerned about the way her daughter speaks — so she's paying for the girl to have electrocution lessons.

Mrs Malaprop doesn't like going upstairs in department stores because she is nervous of travelling on the alligators.

Mrs Malaprop now does her Christmas shopping in November to avoid having to mangle with the terrible crowds.

At one stage Mrs Malaprop used to play the hobo in an orchestra.

♣

Mrs Malaprop's son has just given his girlfriend a well deserved maternity ring.

THE REAL MRS MALAPROP

The real Mrs Malaprop, who was the grape-grape grandmother of our present heroin, first surfaced in 1775 from the pen of Richard Bramley Sheridan in *The Rivals.* Here are some of the original malapropisms that made her famous. Some of these suffer from being out of contact:

But the point we would request of you is that you will promise to forget this fellow, to illiterate him, I say, quite from your memory.

Now don't attempt to extirpate yourself from the matter; you know I have proof of it.

Nay, nay, Sir Anthony you are an absolute misanthropy.

Fie, fie, Sir Anthony, you surely speak laconically.

Well, at any rate I shall be glad to get her from my intuition.

But mind, Lucy, if ever you betray what you are encrusted with (unless it be other people's secrets to me) you forfeit my malevolence for ever.

But from the ingenuity of your appearance, I am convinced you deserve the character here given of you.

He is the very pineapple of politeness.

But, behold, this very day I have interceded another letter from the fellow.

Then he's so well bred, so full of alacrity and adulation.

Well, Sir Anthony, since you desire it, we will not anticipate the past.

That gentleman can tell you — 'twas he enveloped the affair to me.

You have no more feeling than one of the Derbyshire petrifactions.

Why, fly with the utmost felicity.

Nay, no delusions to the past.

Oh, he will dissolve my mystery.

I am as headstrong as an allegory on the banks of the Nile.

Mrs Malaprop's husband has just run off with another woman. She is a victim of the infernal triangle.

For her next summer holiday, Mrs Malaprop has decided to really get away from it all — she is flying to the Soviet Onion.

Mrs Malaprop's nephew and his girlfriend have set up house together. Mrs Malaprop has told them that she does not approve of unmarried people corabbiting together.

The first time Mrs Malaprop saw a nudist she was quite shocked.
'There he was,' she told a friend, 'standing starch naked on the beach.'

Mrs Malaprop is redesigning her house from top to bottom so she has enlisted the services of an inferior decorator.

While in the Middle East Mrs Malaprop was worried that she might get bitten by a mad dog and go down with rabbis.

Even in kindergarten the young Mrs Malaprop showed promise.
Asked what she had learned in school she told her mother 'the bowels, a e i o and u'

♣

MRS MALAPROP ON SCIENCE

Radio was invented by Macaroni.

The thermometer was invented by centipede.

A force 12 torpedo is very destructive.

The amoeba is a one-celled orgasm.

Atoms join together to form monocles.

A triangle with an angle bigger than 90° is obscene.

Each drop of water contains millions of Germans.

The longest side of a right-angled triangle is called a hippopotamus.

Lemons commit mass suicide by jumping over cliffs.

Juniper is the largest of the planets.

MRS MALAPROP ON MEDICINE

The circulatory system contains the veins, archeries and caterpillars.

Consternation is when you haven't been to the toilet for a week.

Bodies are sent to a mortuary to be mortgaged.

Some specialists are eye and rear doctors.

Before birth a mother's womb is diluted.

If you can't eat in hospital you are given inter-avenous feeding.

Just before birth a woman has contraptions.

Many organs in the body have ducks leading from them.

The lungs are comical in shape.

Poisonous wastes leave the body through the rectory.

Some men have to have a prostrate operation.

Mrs Malaprop was reading an article about prostitution and call girls — 'It's not the girls who have to go on the streets who are the cause of the problem,' she declared, 'but the pimples who take all their money.'

Mrs Malaprop has written a serious novel but she doesn't expect it to be published in her lifetime. However, there is a good chance that it may appear posthumorously.

Mrs Malaprop does not get on very well with her next-door neighbour.
    'I don't like her and she doesn't like me,' she says, 'so the feeling is entirely neutral.'

Mrs Malaprop's daughter has recently got married and to her mother's great disappointment the wedding did not take place in church. Instead she was married in one of those off-licence places.

A friend of Mrs Malaprop's has just been rushed to hospital with a serious heart condition. He has a blocked archery.

Mrs Malaprop feels that we should be kind to illiterate children — after all it's not their fault that their parents weren't married.

When the police picked up Mrs Malaprop's son

on suspicion of burglary he had an ali baba that he was somewhere else at the time.

When Mrs Malaprop went out to dinner recently the first item on the menu was the dreaded cutlet.

Mrs Malaprop refuses to commit herself or take any risks on behalf of anybody.

'I'm not putting my head in a moose no matter what is at stake,' she declares.

When Mrs Malaprop was getting married and leaving her office job, all the other girls gave her a little momentum of the occasion.

Recently Mrs Malaprop went to see that wonderful play *Juno and the Paycock* by Seán O'Casey. The line she liked best was 'Joxer, the whole world is in a state of chassis'.

From her study of literature Mrs Malaprop knows that the ancient Greek poets were inspired by the tragic mouse.

Mrs Malaprop has decided to go to Africa for her annual vaccination.

Mrs Malaprop has great sympathy for people in jail. When one escaped recently, she gave him refuse in her house.

Mrs Malaprop has great admiration for storm-troopers who break down doors, rush into buildings and release ostriches.

Mrs Malaprop has difficulty reading old-fashioned timepieces so she has decided to buy one of those new genital watches.

Mrs Malaprop bought an apple recently and was disgusted to find a magnet in it.

Mrs Malaprop's husband has an abbess on his gums which makes eating nearly impossible.

Mrs Malaprop loves an odd drink so she's glad she didn't live in America during proposition.

The first and second things that Mrs Malaprop most wants in life are fame and security, respectably.

Mrs Malaprop was given a present of a lovely new pen for her birthday, so now she can write in hysterics.

Mrs Malaprop's husband is seriously ill. He collapsed and is still in a comma.

Mrs Malaprop had a serious skin complaint but she cured it with one of those ultra-violent lamps.

Mrs Malaprop is the matron saint of all verbal blunderers.

Mrs Malaprop was taking part in a classical quiz. Her first question was: 'What did Socrates die of?'

'That's easy,' she smiled, 'an overdose of wedlock.'

Mrs Malaprop's daughter lost her job as a secretary because of her bad punctuation.

'That's very unjust,' said her mother, 'I know for a fact that she was at work promptly at nine o'clock every morning.'

Mrs Malaprop believes in capital punishment for children in schools as long as it's not too severe.

Mrs Malaprop's next-door neighbour goes in and out to the city to work every day. He's a computer.

Mrs Malaprop went for a walk in the countryside one evening and was nearly eaten alive by midgets. She was sorry she hadn't worn some insect propellant.

Mrs Malaprop's daughter is getting married next week so she is busily preparing her torso.

Mrs Malaprop loves old fashioned novels especially where the hero wears a molecule in his eye.

Mrs Malaprop has just bought a pair of those waterproof knickers just in case she ever goes on the continent.

Mrs Malaprop's advice to those who want to control their figure is to chew each piece of food thirty-two times — masturbate, masturbate, masturbate.

When a man with evil designs on Mrs Malaprop's daughter tried to seduce her, the good girl reclined to do so.

Mrs Malaprop feels that a good public speaker should always breathe with his diagram.

Mrs Malaprop's daughter has just failed her third spelling test in a row. She's afraid she may be anorexic.

Mrs Malaprop's husband is a do-it-yourself enthusiast. There is nothing he likes better than to get his hands on a good solid wench.

Mrs Malaprop's favourite composer is Mozart and she admires him particularly because he was an infant podgy.

Mrs Malaprop is of the opinion that wild beasts should not be confined in theological gardens.

Mrs Malaprop was taken on a tour of a mediaeval church recently. She was very impressed by the flying buttocks in the design.

One of Mrs Malaprop's greatest pleasures in life is to have a giraffe of wine with a good meal.

Mrs Malaprop would like to become an American citizen and since she wasn't born there she will have to become neutralised.

Mrs Malaprop loves sailing on the river and always keeps a boat tied up at the dwarf.

Mrs Malaprop married young in the first fine careless rupture of love.

Mrs Malaprop once went to Canada and was amazed to see all the wide open spaces. She realised that the country is very sparsely copulated.

Mrs Malaprop's train was delayed recently when somebody pulled the excommunication cord.

Mrs Malaprop's son is training to be a doctor. He hopes to become a sturgeon eventually.

MRS MALAPROP'S FAVOURITE MUSIC

Raindrops keep falling on my bed.

Stars and Strikes Forever.

I'm a dreamer, Montreal.

Sam and Janet Evening.

Your Walrus hurt the one you love.

Just a pong at toilet.

Gladly the cross-eyed bear.

While shepherds washed their socks by night.

I left my heart with some franciscans.

Handel's Lager.

Haydn's Cremation.

Verdi's Rectum.

Piddler on the Roof.

Wagner's Ride of the Vultures.

Puccini's Madame Buttermilk.

The Maypole Leaf Forever.

All Teachers Great and Small.

Beethoven's Erotica Symphony.

Rogers and Hammersmith's The Sound of Munich.

South Specific.

Elgar's Enema Variations.

Carry me back to old virginity.

The King and Di.

The Song is ended but the malady lingers on.

O God dour help in ages past.

Verdi's Hyena.

Andrew Lloyd Weber's Ryvita.

Jesus wants me for a sardine.

Debussy's La Mal de Mer.

The Dream of Geronimo.

Rumpelstiltskin's Symphony.

Tarzan Stripes Forever.

Tchaikovsky's Pathetic Symphony.

Ruby Tanyard.

The Star-spangled Banana.

Hairy with the light brown Jeans.

Rock Manninoff.

Can't Get Loose to Using You.

The traffic congestion near Mrs Malaprop's house is unbelievable. She is hoping that the council will build a dual cabbageway.

The wheels have just fallen off the base of Mrs Malaprop's couch. It is very inconvenient pushing a castrated couch around.

Mrs Malaprop feels that the law is too laxative on certain kinds of criminals.

Mrs Malaprop has just bought a new house. It's got a 99 year leash.

What did Mrs Malaprop say when she went to the zoo?
That's irrelevant.

Mrs Malaprop well remembers the end of the Second World War. She threw a VD party in her street.

What is Mrs Malaprop's favourite drink?
Decapitated coffee.

Mrs Malaprop has just installed a beautiful new kitchen. It's even got a spit-level grill.

The income tax authorities claim that Mrs Malaprop owes them over ten thousand pounds in back taxes and she claims that they owe her an equal amount in rebates and both sides refuse to budget.

Mrs Malaprop recently applied for a divorce. She told the judge that her husband often did abdominal things to her in front of her friends.

A few years ago Mrs Malaprop was nearly drowned. A lifeguard rescued her and gave her artificial insemination.

Mrs Malaprop is planning a hunting holiday in Scotland. She is hoping to bag a few peasants.

MR MALAPROP: 'I fancy some eggs for tea, dear.'
MRS MALAPROP: 'I haven't got a single one in the house. How about popping down to the shop and buying a cartoon?'

Mrs Malaprop has just returned from a trip to New York. The most impressive sight she saw was the Vampire State Building.

Mrs Malaprop is thinking of taking up art classes so she has decided to buy a weasel.

Mrs Malaprop's husband never seems to look a day older. He seems to have discovered the secret of eternal euthanasia.

Mrs Malaprop heard that a certain actor was a sexagenarian. Her comment was — 'at his age I think that's disgusting'.

Mrs Malaprop doesn't like universities because young men and women are forced to matriculate together there.

Mrs Malaprop went to the zoo recently. Her favourite animals were the turquoises moving slowly in their cage.

Mrs Malaprop always hopes for the best. She is an eternal octopus.

Mrs Malaprop's daughter has just given birth to a baby. To mark this suspicious event, she has given her a silver tankard.

Mrs Malaprop doesn't want her cat to have any more kittens so she's having it sprayed.

Mrs Malaprop has just been reading about the Kennedy assignation. She believes that the shot was fired by Lee Harvey Oswald from a Dallas Book Suppository.

Mrs Malaprop sometimes finds it difficult to extinguish between different words.

Mrs Malaprop has just been to the chiropodist because she has a bazooka on her foot.

Mrs Malaprop can write with both left and right hands. She is completely amphibious.

Mrs Malaprop is very excited about the new blot of flats being built in her area.

There is a ghost in one of the houses in Mrs Malaprop's street. She feels it should be taken out and exercised.

Mrs Malaprop believes that everybody in the country should have a higher per capital income.

Mrs Malaprop is often in trouble. She always jumps from the pancake into the frying pan.

Mrs Malaprop has a complaint against the government. She's going to write to the ombugsman.

Mrs Malaprop has just bought an expensive new pet — it's a filigree hamster.

Mrs Malaprop has just returned from Scotland with a lovely new coat made of haggis tweed.

Mrs Malaprop just doesn't know what to do. She is in a complete quarry.

Mrs Malaprop loves her old gramophone and her old 78 records. She doesn't hold with these new compost discs at all.

Mrs Malaprop's nephew is a monk. He has just celibated the twenty-fifth anniversary of his ordination.

Mrs Malaprop has decided to change her will, so she is going to ask her solicitor to add a cul-de-sac to it.

Mrs Malaprop was asked to nominate her favourite President of the United States. Without hesitation she replied 'PLJ'.

Mrs Malaprop's doctor has diagnosed that she is suffering from digestive problems and her nerves. She is thinking of taking up transcendental medication and yogurt.

Mrs Malaprop's son is a very saintly fellow. She feels he may even have a vacation to the priesthood.

Mrs Malaprop was asked in a quiz to name the prime minister of Cuba. Without hesitation she replied 'Fidel Castrato'.

Mrs Malaprop's husband has worked for the government for many years. He's a senile servant.

Mrs Malaprop's dog has just had a litre of puppies.

Mrs Malaprop has just been to the zoo where she saw a rhinostrich.

Mrs Malaprop has just bought a lovely new car. It's a blue hunchback.

Mrs Malaprop remained single until she was nearly thirty. Then she entered into the state of holy acrimony.

♣

MALAPROPS IN SHAKESPEARE

Sheridan of course was not the first writer to employ malapropisms. In *Much Ado About Nothing* old Bill Jakesbeer himself had a character, a constable named Dogberry, who dropped verbal clangers. However, Dogberry's efforts, with one notable exception, were rather contrived and not very funny. It is fortunate that the name didn't stick or now you would be reading a book of dogberries, which sound a little like some foul canine intestinal disorder. Here, for the record, are a few of Dogberry's malapropisms:

You are thought here to be the most senseless and fit man for the constable of the watch.

For the watch to babble and to talk is most tolerable and not to be endured.

Adieu; be vigitant, I beseech you.

Comparisons are odorous.

Our watch sir, have indeed comprehended two aspicious persons.

It shall be suffigance.

Only get the learned writer to set down our excommunication.

Is the whole dissembly appeared?

O villain! thou wilt be condemn'd into everlasting redemption for this.

Dost thou not suspect my place? Dost thou not suspect my years?

By this time our sexton hath reformed Signior Leonato of the matter.

And if a merry meeting may be wished, God prohibit it!

Mrs Malaprop's favourite perfume is odour cologne.

Mrs Malaprop claims there are two types of forest — carnivorous and insidious.

Mrs Malaprop hates being the skateboard of other people's mistakes.

As a little girl during the war Mrs Malaprop was evaporated to the countryside.

Mrs Malaprop's washing machine has broken down because somebody threw a spaniel in the works.

Mrs Malaprop has just applied to her local health authority for a disability benefit. They sent her a bluff form to fill in.

One of Mrs Malaprop's cousins works for the government. He's a civil serpent.

Mrs Malaprop checks prices at her local supermarket every week. She is amazed at the way baked beans flatulate.

When Mrs Malaprop went to have an x-ray she was told to change her clothes in a cuticle.

When Mrs Malaprop was at sea recently she was lucky enough to see a shawl of herrings.

Mr Malaprop does not take sandwiches to work anymore. He uses luncheon vultures instead.

Mrs Malaprop was given one of these new fountain pens but she doesn't use it because she hates messing about with cartilages.

One of Mrs Malaprop's favourite sights is a deacon on a hill with a fire on top.

Mrs Malaprop's little nephew was always getting ill, so they took him in to hospital to have his asteroids taken out.

Mrs Malaprop attended a wedding recently. She thought that the bribe and the gloom looked beautiful.

Mrs Malaprop doesn't use much make-up. She likes just a little massacre on her eyes.

Sometimes for a special treat, Mrs Malaprop gives her family a delightful desert — Neopolitician ice cream.

Mrs Malaprop is buying a new car on higher purchase. She's never had anything on the extortion plan before.

Mrs Malaprop's son joined the army. She boasted that he was promoted to the rank of court-marshal after only a few weeks.

Mrs Malaprop is very worried about dust in the air in case she gets a foreigner's body in her eye.

Mrs Malaprop's father was an old soldier who attained the rank of corpuscle.

Mrs Malaprop is not too keen on sunbathing. She's afraid of the sun's ultra-violent rays.

Mrs Malaprop is glad to hear that the miners' strike has been settled by holding a ballet at each of the pits.

Mrs Malaprop couldn't figure out what she was getting for her birthday but she worked it out by a process of illumination.

Mrs Malaprop always boils water before drinking it in order to putrefy it.

When Mrs Malaprop is writing a letter she likes to leave a one inch virgin on the left hand side of each page.

Mrs Malaprop was introducing her future son-in-law to her friends.
    'This is my daughter's fiasco,' she announced.

Mrs Malaprop would love to visit the uninhibited parts of the world.

Mrs Malaprop remembers when her children were in nappies, but as she says herself, 'we've all passed a lot of water since then.'

Mrs Malaprop believes that the most effective form of combat in the jungle is gorilla warfare.

MRS MALAPROP ON FRANCE

The highest peak in the Alps is Blanc Mange.

The French national anthem is the mayonnaise.

The Awful Tower is in Paris.

French coalmen deliver fuel coal de sack or á la carte.

French people live in gateaux.

French cities are full of burglars.

French houses are made of plaster of Paris.

The French are always having general erections.

MRS MALAPROP ON ITALY

Italian babies are called bamboos.

There is a famous leaning tower in Pizza.

Italy lies in the temperance zone.

Malt and larva run down from the sides of Mound Edna.

In Venus they travel about in gladiolas.

Florence and Nipples are close together.

MRS MALAPROP ON GEOGRAPHY

The Mediterranean and the Red Sea are connected by the Sewage Canal.

The Pyramids are a range of mountains between France and Spain.

Egyptian fields are irritated by the Nile.

America was discovered by Columbanus.

The Urinal mountains are in Russia.

Hot parts of the world are called the horrid zones.

The people of the frozen north are called equinoxes.

It is very hot in the topical regions of the world.

The people of Malta are called Maltesers.

The Pyjamas are islands in the Atlantic Ocean.

The abdominal snowman is found in Tibet.

The path of the earth around the sun is an eclipse.

Much of the world's rubber is produced in malaria.

The inhabitants of Moscow are called mosquitoes.

Plasticine is a country in the Middle East.

The seaport of Athens is called the pyorrhoea.

The world's greatest ocean is the Specific Ocean.

The line around the middle of the earth is called the creator.

In China people ride around in jigsaws.

Manila is the capital of the Philistines.

In Danish they have omelettes on some letters.

The Mongrels live in part of China.

The earth makes a resolution every twenty-four hours.

Milligan was the first man to sail around the world.

In India people are divided into casts and out-casts.

The tallest building in the world is the Umpire State.

The rubble is the unit of currency in Russia.

Japanese girls dress in commodes.

Mrs Malaprop's favourite footballer was crapped for England seventeen times.

Mrs Malaprop is forever reading the Old Testament — she's a regular bibliomaniac.

Mrs Malaprop has just visited the west of Ireland to the spot where Alcock and Bull landed in their aeroplane after crossing the Atlantic.

Mrs Malaprop dislikes double glazing because it gives rise to too much compensation.

One of Mrs Malaprop's favourite historical characters is the Duck of Wellington.

There is nothing Mrs Malaprop likes more than a day in the country with a full picnic hamster.

Mrs Malaprop doesn't believe what her next door neighbour tells her. She thinks you've got to take everything the woman says with a dose of salts.

Mrs Malaprop loves her new word processor and finds the curser particularly useful.

The first intimidation Mrs Malaprop received that she had to go to court was when a policeman knocked on her door.

Once Mrs Malaprop was taken short in the street and had to use a public conveyance.

Mrs Malaprop is very particular about what kind of bed she sleeps on. She always demands an inferior spring mattress.

Mrs Malaprop is very concerned about the damage caused by tropical typhoid storms.

One of Mrs Malaprop's favourite presidents of the United States of America is Franklin Delaney Roosevelt.

One of Mrs Malaprop's consolations is to have a husband to shave all the enjoyable things in life.

Mrs Malaprop's uncle has just died and she has been invited to be a polar bear at the funeral.

Mrs Malaprop has just been reading about a dreadful disease called sleeping sickness which is brought on by the bite of the sexy fly.

Mrs Malaprop has been reading a Swedish book on sexual self-discovery. Now she knows where her volvo is.

Because of all the recent scares about consumer terrorism, Mrs Malaprop never buys anything in a supermarket unless it is helmetically sealed.

Mrs Malaprop was asked in a quiz who the Emperor of Ethiopia was. Without hesitation she replied: 'Highly's a Lassie.'

Mrs Malaprop's artistic nephew has just got a job with a publishing firm as a poof reader.

Mrs Malaprop's favourite poet is Wordsworth because he was always answering the call of nature.

Mrs Malaprop was asked what her favourite religion was — 'The Quackers,' she replied.

Mrs Malaprop is plagued by aunts in her house. She is going to ask the chemist to give her something to get rid of them.

When Mrs Malaprop's grandfather joined the

army many years ago he couldn't decide between the calvary or the infamy.

Mrs Malaprop remembers as a little girl during the war listening to the radio broadcasts of Lord Hee-Haw.

Who is Mrs Malaprop's favourite Scottish poet? Rabbi Burns.

Mrs Malaprop thinks that the patron saint of animals is St Francis of Onassis.

When people point out her blunders to her, it really gets Mrs Malaprop's gander up.

Mrs Malaprop is going to write a novel — she already has the mucus of a good plot.

Mrs Malaprop doesn't really like foreigners but she had no objection when her daughter became engaged to an Arabian shriek with lots of money.

Mrs Malaprop has just started studying philosophy. She likes best of all Pluto, the ancient Greek.

Mrs Malaprop does not approve of the permissive society. She is totally opposed to all immortal behaviour.

Mrs Malaprop and her husband have decided to build a conservative beside their house.

Mrs Malaprop has just filled in her income tax and sent it to the Inspector of Texas.

Mrs Malaprop is having some workmen in for altercations.

Mrs Malaprop admits that she is inclined to make the odd foxes pass.

Mrs Malaprop is applying for a divorce because her marriage has never been consumed.

Mrs Malaprop does not approve of the effluent society because they are stinking rich. Nor does she approve of people with the odour of sanctity — they stick to high heaven.

One of Mrs Malaprop's favourite buildings is St Paul's Cathedral designed by Sir Christopher Robin.

Mrs Malaprop is very interested in the space race. She watches every launch from Cape Carnival.

Mrs Malaprop has an upset stomach. She is afraid it may be a billiards attack.

♣

What sort of car does Mrs Malaprop
drive?
A fait accompli.

MRS MALAPROP ON RELIGION AGAIN

John the Baptist was beheaded with the Axe of the Apostles.

Agnes Dei was the mother of God.

The principal religion of China is confusionism.

Our Father, who art in Heaven, Harold by thy name.

The kodak is the Muslim bible.

The members of the Church of Latterday Saints are known as morons.

The pope declared Luther's teaching to be hereditary.

The 23rd Sam: Surely good Mrs Murphy shall follow me all the days of my life and I will dwell in the house of the Lord forever.

Lead us not into Thames Station.

The Geneva Witnesses are a religious sect.

At Pentecost, God sent us the Holy Goat.

The Utilitarian Church is of recent origin.

A Seminary is where priests bury their dead.

People who are not Jews are called reptiles.

The Vergil Mary was the mother of Jesus.

A vixen is the wife of a vicar.

Jacob had a brother called See-Saw.

Blessed are the cheesemakers.

Jesus had twelve opossums.

The Authorised Virgin is the best translation of the bible.

Alias was one of the sons of Abraham.

You cannot serve God and Mamma.

Protestants dislike the smell of incest in Catholic churches.

They came to Jesus carrying a parable on a bed.

The first long-distance runner in the Bible was the good Sam Marathon.

Mrs Malaprop once met the Irish Prime Minister, the teeshirt.

Mrs Malaprop has become very health conscious. She won't eat any food that has got conservatives in it.

Mrs Malaprop is very interested in Russian history. She loves reading about the Bazzar of Russia and his children the Sardines.

Mrs Malaprop has just planted some beautiful flowers in her garden. They are called scabies.

Mrs Malaprop loves the flavour of orange but finds that oranges are very expensive — so she makes do with consecrated orange juice instead.

Mrs Malaprop just loves the way that Indian squaws carry porpoises and squawkers on their backs.

What is Mrs Malaprop's favourite underwear? Her Freudian slip.

Mrs Malaprop has just cut her hand with a silver of glass.

Mrs Malaprop is about to have a serious operation, but she has every confidence in the atheist who will put her to sleep.

Mrs Malaprop's daughter has just walked down the isle.

Before Mrs Malaprop's baby was born she attended an anti-naval clinic.

Mrs Malaprop has just been to see a specialist. He has told her that she has cadillacs on her eyes.

Mrs Malaprop is into alternative medicine. She is even thinking of having acupulco but she doesn't fancy having all those needles stuck in her.

Some children came to Mrs Malaprop's door the other evening collecting for bombfires night.

Two of Mrs Malaprop's favourite comedians are Rabbit and Costello.

Mrs Malaprop enjoyed herself so much in church one Sunday that she went round to the clergyman afterwards and said to him 'that was a wonderful sermon you preached. Every word of it was absolutely superfluous'.

Mrs Malaprop is learning how to save people from drowning by artificial perspiration.

♣

MRS MALAPROP ON HISTORY

Mussolini's followers were facetious.

Mary Queen of Scots married the Dolphin of France.

The constitution of the United States of America gives everyone the right to bare arms.

The German Emperor was called the Geyser.

Anne Berlin was the wife of Henry VIII.

Sir Francis Drake said the Armada could wait but his bowels couldn't.

Henry the Eighth's marriage was dull and void.

Napoleon was imprisoned on the island of Melba.

The motto of the French Revolution was Liberty, Equality, Maternity.

One of the most famous kings of England was William the Conjuror.

Henry the Eighth married Catherine of Arrogance and Anne of Cloves.

Louis XVI was gelatined during the French Revolution.

Napoleon had no children because Josephine was a baroness.

Queen Victoria was the longest serving souvenir England ever had.

Mary Queen of Spots became Queen of England.

Cleopatra was bitten on the arm by a wasp.

Magna Carta — did she die in vain?

Columbus circumcised the world with a forty foot clipper

The Crusaders overcame the Saccharins.

When Mrs Malaprop's daughter was married all the guests threw graffiti at the bride.

Mrs Malaprop joined the local fencing club. She objected to the fact that she had to pay a decapitation fee.

Mrs Malaprop's husband has just bought her a new waist disposal system.

Mrs Malaprop feels we should all eat cheese because the first man in the Bible was called Edam.

Mrs Malaprop has just been elected secretary of a local organisation. Her first task is to make out a gender for the opening meeting.

Mrs Malaprop loves seafood. Last time she dined out she had a portion of scimpi.

Mrs Malaprop doesn't like the rumours being brandied about that she drinks too much.

From Mrs Malaprop's album of favourite music — 'The slurry with the fridge on top'.

When Mrs Malaprop's friend was in hospital with a serious illness she brought her some flowers to improve her morals.

Mrs Malaprop thinks it is disgraceful how some men live off their wives' immortal earnings.

Mrs Malaprop was reading the other night about Stanley's African exploration and the famous meeting where he uttered the words 'Ken Livingstone I presume'.

Mrs Malaprop's niece hopes to become an opera singer. She plans to make her debut at Convent Garden.

After her marriage, Mrs Malaprop had an exciting wedding conception.

Mrs Malaprop has just made extensive altercations to her house. For example, she has just
installed new tubercular lighting.

Mrs Malaprop excuses her verbal lapses by say-
ing that most of the time she is metamorp-
hically speaking.

Mrs Malaprop's teenage son uses a lot of bad
language but she thinks it's just a phrase he's
going through.

Mrs Malaprop is a strong believer in the next
life. However, she doesn't know if she is going
to heaven, hell, or puberty.

Mrs Malaprop now does all her business at her
local supermarket and not at the corner shop.
She thinks the prices there are very exuberant.

Mrs Malaprop used to wear pyjamas but recently
she has taken to wearing a negligent.

Mrs Malaprop has just been reading that in
some parts of the world there is detention without trial. She thinks that is a fragrant violation
of human rights.

Among Mrs Malaprop's very favourite pieces of
music is 'The Blue Daniel'.

♣

NURSERY RHYMES

When they were little, Mrs Malaprop's children liked her to read nursery rhymes to them. They grew up learning the following lines:

London breeches falling down.

Diddle diddle dumpling mice on John.

She cut off their tails with a carbon knife.

The Pied Piper of Hamlet.

There was a little girl and she had a little curl
Right in the middle of her forest.

Little Miss Muffet sat on a tuffet
Eating her curves away.

The Three Little Prigs.

Walt Disney's Scampi.

Dick Whittington and his Cap.

Mary, Mary quiet and hairy.

One for the bastard and one for the dame.

Mrs Malaprop is very worried about the spectrum of nuclear war hanging over the world.

From time to time Mrs Malaprop likes to play the guitar. She thinks it's got something to do with her minstrel cycle.

Mrs Malaprop's son has just gone to America but she hopes to be incommunicado with him soon.

Mrs Malaprop will never forget her wedding day. The highlight of the ceremony was when her husband-to-be was asked 'do you take this woman to be your awful wedded wife?'

Mrs Malaprop's daughter went to France and is now expecting a baby. Her mother is not passing any judgment until she hears her virgin of the story.

Mrs Malaprop didn't think she could have any children because her husband was impudent.

When Mrs Malaprop visited Australia recently, the animals she liked most were the cola bears and the aubergines.

One of Mrs Malaprop's favourite dishes is cheese on toast heated under the gorilla.

Mrs Malaprop was convinced that she had completed her family, that she was impregnable and that it was inconceivable that she should ever have another baby.

Yet there were certain symptoms — she hadn't demonstrated for three months so she felt she might be stagnant.

So she went to the doctor who tested her, but the test confirmed that Mrs Malaprop was going through the metal pause and he suggested that she have her aviaries removed.

However, it was finally discovered that Mrs Malaprop was just endemic because she didn't have enough red corkscrews in her blood-stream.

Later, to everyone's surprise, she found that she was pregnant.

The doctor advised her to have a cistercian section but she decided to go for the epiduracell method instead.

As it turned out, the midwife had to use her biceps to deliver the baby.

♣

Mrs Malaprop was reading the other day about how the cotton crop in the deep south is ruined by the bold weasel.

Mrs Malaprop is thinking of changing her religion. She's going to become a Seventh Day Adventurer.

Mrs Malaprop was lustily singing a Christmas carol:
   A weigh in a manger, no crib for a bed,
   The little lord Jesus, laid down his wee Ted.

Mrs Malaprop is thinking of buying a lovely old house with ivory growing up the walls.

One of Mrs Malaprop's nephews has acme all over his face.

Mrs Malaprop feels that Jesus should have been released instead of Brer Rabbit.

When Mrs Malaprop is in town she loves to have lunch and a glass of wine in a brassiere.

At her wedding, Mrs Malaprop displayed her new 22-carrot gold ring.

Mrs Malaprop's favourite flowers are coronations.

Mrs. Malaprop's favourite poet is Keats and her very favourite line is — Season of mists and melon fruitfulness.

Mrs Malaprop's son was married in an old fashioned ceremony. He said to his wife-to-be 'to thee I pledge my trough'.

What is Mrs Malaprop's favourite fast food? Hamburglars!

When Mrs Malaprop eats, all her food passes through her elementary canal.

Mrs Malaprop has a severe pain in her chest. She's afraid she may have angela.

Mrs Malaprop's patron saint is St Samuel a Beckett.

Mrs Malaprop's son has lots of girlfriends. He's a regular Don Coyote.

Mrs Malaprop was reading the other night about the French Revolution and in particular how Marie and Toinette said, 'You can't have your cake and eat it'.

Mrs Malaprop is not looking forward to the end of the world. She is terrified of Agamemnon.

Mrs Malaprop was reading in the newspapers how robbers got away with a huge amount of gold billion.

Mrs Malaprop has taken up sailing and she has bought a dingy boat.

Mrs Malaprop was surprised to learn that one of the most popular christian names in Poland is Santa Claus.

Mrs Malaprop is having dental trouble so she is going to get falsetto teeth.

Mrs Malaprop's most abiding memory of Spain is seeing the natives dancing the flamingo.

Mrs Malaprop's daughter is getting married and she feels a strange infinity with her.

One of Mrs Malaprop's favourite prayers is the Angus Dei.

Mrs Malaprop is seriously ill. The doctors have diagnosed double ammonia.

Mrs Malaprop's husband has just got a job in a market garden at a celery of £15,000 a year.

Mrs Malaprop believes that the nuclear arms race should end. For a start there should be a ban on the production of geranium.

Mrs Malaprop is pretty fat. In the opinion of some, she is obeast.

Mrs Malaprop loves watching wrestling and judy on the television.

Mrs Malaprop was chairperson at a meeting. It became so rowdy that she had to bang her gravel on the desk.

One of Mrs Malaprop's favourite days of the year is the feast of All Hollows.

Mrs Malaprop hates cruelty to animals. If animals have to be killed, she believes it should be done with a human killer.

Mrs Malaprop's grandfather could neither read nor write. He was completely illegitimate.

Mrs Malaprop went to a restaurant one night but found that the food was completely indelible.

Mrs Malaprop does not believe that any man should have more than one wife. She supports mahogany.

Mrs Malaprop has inconvertible evidence about the identity of Jack the Ripper.

Mrs Malaprop's favourite Christmas carol is Silent Night, Deadly Night.

When Mrs Malaprop first saw a snake she was absolutely putrefied.

♣

MRS MALAPROP'S FAVOURITE LITERATURE

Withering Heights.

Touchdown in As You Like It.

Gray's Allergy.

Shakespeare's Merry Widow.

Tess of the Dormobiles.

Robinson Caruso.

Desdemona, who played the trumpet in Othello's bed.

The Scarlet Litter.

Long John Hitler.

Vergil's Aniseed or Vergil's Enid.

Orwell's Dining out in London and Paris.

Fellatio — Hamlet's best friend.

Tennyson's In Memorandum.

Milton's Paradise Lust.

Shelley's Ode to a Skylight.

Titus and Ronicus.

Darwin's Organ of the Spices.

Wordsworth's Imitations of Immorality.

Homer's Oddity.

Laurence of Olivier.

Gray's Effigy.

Romeo and Juliet – the heroic couplet.

Omelette, Prince of Denmark.

The Lion, the Bitch and the Wardrobe.

101 Damnations.

Little Louse on the Prairie.

Agatha Christie's Witness for the Prostitution.

Pope's Heroic Cutlets.

Honky-Tonk Expedition.

The Count of Monte Carlo.

James Joyce's Useless.

Cot on a Hot Tin Roof.

Robinson Caruso's Good Friday.

Adolph Hitler's Mine Cramp.

One of the highlights of Mrs Malaprop's trip to Russia was her visit to the gremlin.

If there was one rule Mrs Malaprop learned in school, it was 'never end a sentence with a proposition'.

When Mrs Malaprop was attacked by a mugger recently, she kept her composer throughout the incident.

Mrs Malaprop gets this strange feeling when great events are about to happen. She thinks she may be sidekick.

When Mrs Malaprop went to Egypt she saw the Stinks in the desert.

For name tags Mrs Malaprop always uses incredible ink.

When Mrs Malaprop was ill recently the doctor injected her with peninsula.

When Mrs Malaprop was travelling through the jungle she was attacked by a boa constructor.

A couple of Mrs Malaprop's favourite lines from Shakespeare, the bird of Avon —
Bubble, bubble, toilet trouble;

Beware the brides of March.

While on the beach, there is nothing Mrs Malaprop likes more than to see sunbathers basketing in the sun.

Mrs Malaprop picked up her latest outfit at a rembrandt sale.

Mrs Malaprop really misses the services of her recently diseased husband.

Mrs Malaprop is really looking forward to the next government wipe paper.

Mrs Malaprop was attacked by a mugger and beaten subconscious.

Mrs Malaprop's telephone broke down and she had to use the local chaos in her village.

Mrs Malaprop thinks her husband is too amorous. In fact she feels he's a sex-mechanic.

Mrs Malaprop's nephew has just got a job at the airport. He's been assigned to the customs and exercise division.

Mrs Malaprop has just been to an art gallery where she was viewing the mantlepieces of the great masters.

Mrs Malaprop has recently been reading the great classics of Greek mythology. Her favourite story concerns Achilles' mother who dipped him in the River Stinks.

Mrs Malaprop once took up chess as a hobby but gave it up after only a few weeks. She never even learned to move her prawns properly.

One of Mrs Malaprop's favourite political moments of the year is when the Minister for Finance presents his budgie to the nation.

Mrs Malaprop on the number of wives a man should have:

One wife, that's monotony;
Two wives, that's bigotry;
Three wives, that's trigonometry.

When Mrs Malaprop got married she wanted some time off work to go on her honeymoon. She applied for some passionate leave.

What is Mrs Malaprop's favourite dish?
Roast lion of pork.

Mrs Malaprop is very afraid that her husband may die suddenly so she has just taken out one of those endearment policies for him.

Mrs Malaprop has just been reading in the newspapers that the police have just uncovered a hugh catch of Carmelite rifles.

Mrs Malaprop is just about to have a blood test and she is very worried in case she turns out to be VIP positive.

Mrs Malaprop was on her holidays in Greece and was shocked because nudist bathing was allowed on the pubic beaches.

Mrs Malaprop's son teaches at the university. 'He's a lecherer in sociology,' she tells people proudly.

Mrs Malaprop found a fly in her soup in a restaurant so naturally she complained and asked to speak to the manager. He told her it must have committed insecticide.

Mrs Malaprop was watching a pirate film on television the other night. She saw a gunboat fire a warning shot across the bowels.

Mrs Malaprop's favourite ancient Greek legend is the saga of Jason and the Astronauts in search of the Golden Fleas.

When Mrs Malaprop's husband returned home late the other night he was completely gin-coherent.

Mrs Malaprop does not approve of the arms' race. For example, she does not think there should be incontinent ballistic missiles.

Mrs Malaprop is worried about her eighteen year old son who has just got married while at university. He is suffering from premature matriculation.

Mrs Malaprop has completed her family so she is going to have a tubal litigation.

Mrs Malaprop has been reading about a Japanese businessman who got into financial difficulties. He committed cash and carry.

Mrs Malaprop's husband was driving home the other night when the police stopped him and asked him to blow into the brotheliser.

Mrs Malaprop cannot take sugar in any shape or form. She is a diabolic.

Mrs Malaprop cannot swallow anything at the moment because her throat is in flames.

Mrs Malaprop was reading the other day about how the body achieves control of the natural functions by means of a spinster.

Mrs Malaprop's brother is a diabetic because his St Pancras has ceased to function.

Because of her fame, there are plans to erect a plague on Mrs Malaprop's house.

When Mrs Malaprop was getting married, she carried a bunch of her favourite flowers — enemas.

Mrs Malaprop ate two dozen oysters and got selfish poisoning.

Mrs Malaprop is an enthusiastic music follower. She never misses the Last Night of the Poms.

Mrs Malaprop loves watching awards on television — her favourite is the Enema Awards.

Mrs Malaprop has just visited the Tower of London.She saw the beefburgers holding halibuts in their hands.

Mrs Malaprop is a golf widow. She complains that her husband never leaves the golf curse.

Mrs Malaprop is very proud of her son. He's just been made a perfect at his school.

Mrs Malaprop has just bought an expensive new table made entirely of monogamy.

One of Mrs Malaprop's happiest memories of her courtship is sitting on couch canoeing with her boyfriend.

Mrs Malaprop has just bought a beautiful new dress. It's covered with thousands of sequences.

When Mrs Malaprop is cooking she likes to use a lot of desecrated coconut.

One of Mrs Malaprop's favourite authors is the Venereal Bede.

Mrs Malaprop's favourite football team were recently regulated from division one.

One of Mrs Malaprop's favourite snacks is cream cheese with a beagle.

Mrs Malaprop has just acquired a lovely new dog. It's a datsun.

Mrs Malaprop has just been reading about superstitious customs in ancient times. It seems that people used to wear omelettes around their necks to ward off evil spirits.

Mrs Malaprop's cousin is a sealic and has to have a glutton free diet.

Mrs Malaprop believes that doctors are producing new inflammation on arthritis all the time.

Before Mrs Malaprop opens a self-assembly kit she always reads the destructions first.

On mornings when Mrs Malaprop is feeling happy she slides down the barristers.

Mr Malaprop was so good on his honeymoon that his wife gave him a standing ovulation.

Mrs Malaprop loves putting explanation marks at the end of sentences.

When she was getting married, Mrs Malaprop's bouquet was a clump of friesians.

Mrs Malaprop has been reading the latest murder sadistics in the newspapers.

Mrs Malaprop has just discovered that her antique Chinese vase dates from the Ming dysentery.

Mrs Malaprop's very favourite opera is Bidet's Carmen.

Before any list of candidates is interviewed, Mrs Malaprop believes that a screaming committee should be set up.

From Mrs Malaprop's list of favourite films – Elizabeth Vagina.

Mrs Malaprop's twin grandchildren are very muck alike. She says they are just like two peas in a pot.

Mrs Malaprop is very upset because the interest rate on her bank loan has risen to 20% per anum (sick).

When Mrs Malaprop has been reading a biography of the famous Russian leader – Joe Stallion.

When Mrs Malaprop has a digestive upset she always takes Milk of Amnesia.

Mrs Malaprop's favourite Italian film star is Gina Lollobrigadier.

When on holiday Mrs Malaprop always brings a rubber sheet with her in case she becomes incompetent.

Mrs Malaprop is fed up of making beds so she is getting rid of all her blankets and buying bidets.

Mrs Malaprop cannot hear a word of the sermon in church because of the poor quality of the agnostics.

Mrs Malaprop's father was injured during the war when he was hit by a piece of sharpnel.

Mrs Malaprop sometimes plays Scrabble just to relieve the monopoly.

Mrs Malaprop is disgusted at the behaviour of the Iraqi leader Soddhim Insane.

One of Mrs Malaprop's favourite jazz singers is Elephants Gerald.

Mrs Malaprop's favourite scene from *Hamlet* is where Polonius is stabbed in the arse.

Mrs Malaprop distrusts doctors so she is consulting a fake healer.

MORE INTERESTING TITLES

THE BOOK OF IRISH BULL
Des MacHale

THE BUMPER BOOK OF KERRYMAN JOKES
Des MacHale

THE LAST OF THE KERRYMAN JOKES
Des MacHale

THE BOOK OF CORKMAN JOKES
Des MacHale

THE BOOK OF IRISH LOVE AND MARRIAGE JOKES
Des MacHale

THE BOOK OF KERRYMAN RIDDLES
Sonnie O'Reilly

THE BOOK OF KERRYWOMAN JOKES
Laura Stack

THE BOOK OF DUBLINMAN JOKES
Y.M. Hughes